HOW TO PLAY THE
Button Accordion & Song Book

Nic "Pennsylvania" Landon

To access audio visit:
www.halleonard.com/mylibrary

Enter Code
4516-9191-0736-0514

ISBN 978-1-57424-416-8
SAN 683-8022

Cover by James Creative Group

Copyright © 2023 CENTERSTREAM Publishing
P.O. Box 17878 - Anaheim Hills, CA 92817

www.centerstream-usa.com | centerstrm@aol.com | 714-779-9390

All rights for publication and distribution are reserved.
No part of this book may be reproduced in any form or by any Electronic or mechanical means including information storage and retrieval systems without permission in writing from the publisher, except by reviewers who may quote brief passages in review.

This book is no way intended to infringe on the intellectual property rights of any party. All products, brands and names represented are trademarks or registered trademarks of their respective companies; information in this book was derived from the author's independent research and was not authorized, furnished or approved by other parties.

Contents

Preface 4
- Thank You 4
- My Accordion Journey 4

The Button Accordion 5
- The Accordion 5
- Bass and Chords 6
- On the Tab 7
- Major Scales 8
- Crossing the Rows 8
- The First Song 10
- A Few Notes on Music and Practicing 10

The First 10 Songs 11
- *Soldier's Joy* 12
- *Spotted Pony* 13
- *Liberty* 14
- *Angelina Baker* 15
- *Devil's Dream* 16
- *Needle Case* 17
- *Arkansas Traveler* 18
- *Whiskey Before Breakfast* 19
- *Over the Waterfall* 20
- *June Apple* 21

Making Your Own Arrangements 22
- Building the Melody 22
- Playing in Two Octaves 24
- *Mississippi Sawyer* 25
- Harmonizing Notes 27
- Providing Backup 28
- *In the Pines* 30

Moving Forward/More Songs 32
- *The Blacksmith* 32
- *Buttermilk & Cider* 33
- *Dubuque* 34
- *Forked Deer* 35
- *Hang On* 36
- *Lamplighter's Hornpipe* 37
- *League & Slasher Reel* 38
- *Little Hornpipe* 39
- *Sweet Ellen* 40
- *Lady on the Railroad* 41
- *Breaking Up Christmas* 42
- *Snowflake Hornpipe* 43
- *Snouts & Ears of America* 44
- *Young America Hornpipe* 45
- *Whiskey* 46
- *Bunch of Keys* 47

Jigs & Waltzes 48
- The Left-hand Waltz Pattern 48
- Counting in 6/8 48
- *The Kesh Jig* 49
- *John Newgrant* 50
- *St. Lawrence Jig* 51
- *The Merry Widow* 52
- *Amazing Grace* 53

Conclusion 54

Thank You

This book would not exist without Ron Pivovar and the fine people at *The National Button Accordion Festival*. It was my attendance at this festival some years ago that inspired me to take the plunge and acquire a button accordion. There have been other encouraging voices that have helped along the way including Scott Bellinger, David Caron, Kari Zeigler, and Blake Ketchum. Emily, my wife, has reminded me that she should also be recognized, not just for her family's history in America's accordion culture, but also for enduring hours of my practicing.

I'm excited to have the opportunity to have this book published by Centerstream, as they have released invaluable books on musical history and styles. I will forever be thankful for my conversations with, and encouragement from, Ron Middlebrook at Centerstream.

Lastly, I would like to thank you for purchasing this book. Whether you be brand new to the instrument or a confident player, I hope that there are rewarding challenges and insights in the pages ahead.

My Accordion Journey

The button accordion's history goes back to the early/mid-19th century. While the piano accordion is today more widely recognized, it did not come about until some decades later. The accordion's volume and portability made it popular in the days before amplification, and different cultures adopted the instrument to suit their music. This led to further design evolution to the point where saying "button accordion" is inadequate, as there are vastly different instruments that fall under the term.

As people immigrated to North America, they brought the accordion with them. The instrument would also be adopted by cultures already present in the New World.

As a child born in a Louisiana, which was seeing a renewed interest in Cajun culture, I saw and heard the iconic one-row boxes most associated with the music they make. Moving to Pennsylvania as a child, I would see the large three, four, and even five row (!) button boxes used by Slovenian groups.

I've been an Old-Time banjo player for years. I've also been a private music instructor for more than a decade. When I finally picked up a button accordion, I was instructed to learn songs I already knew. With that good advice, I decided to figure out how to play the songs I knew on the banjo and mandolin.

When I say *Old-Time*, I am specifically speaking about the string band music associated with Appalachia. While there is a history of accordions in the region, the popular development of Old-Time eschewed many musical cultures that were not English-speaking. It was not until the late 1960s that the Cajun and Norteño began to make inroads to English-speaking traditional music fans.

For more on this history, I recommend Bruce Triggs' seminal book *Accordion Revolution: A People's History of the Accordion in North America from the Industrial Revolution to Rock 'n' Roll*.

The thoughts and arrangements in this book are my own, arrived at after spending years working with the instrument. The exact way I play the instrument continues to evolve as I progress as a player. Consider these arrangements as a springboard. Do not be afraid to deviate from what is on the paper, as long as what you are playing works for you and the song.

The Button Accordion

Button accordions (AKA "melodeons") come in many forms. The most common tend to be the one-row box, the two-row tuned a fourth apart, the two-row semitone box, and the three-row. This book is written with the two-row boxes, tuned a fourth apart, in mind. That said, many of the songs herein can be played on a one-row box.

Because I play many Old-Time tunes, I selected an A/D box. This enables me to easily play in the common keys of A and D, but also G, albeit it with some increased effort and creativity. In England, boxes tuned D/G are preferred. C/F and G/C boxes are also common. The songs in this book are written in A, D, and G, but they can be played on whatever key box that you have. The layout and theory remains the same despite the keys.

Regardless what key your box is in, the right-hand side consists of 21 buttons, located on the top of image A. These are the treble or melody buttons which are played with the right hand. With an A/D box, the outside row corresponds to the notes in the key of A. If you have a C/F box, that outside row will be notes in the key of C. The 10 buttons that make up the A/D box's inside row are the key of D. Again, if you have a C/F box, that inside row will be in the key of F.

Because the boxes are diatonic, meaning each row is one key, they have some inherent limitations. All instruments have some limitations though, and do not let this discourage you as there is a lifetime worth of music in any box.

A final word on tuning... some boxes will have accidentals on the first button in each right-hand row. This provides some additional flexibility. An A/D box with accidental buttons will have extra notes that are outside the A and D scales. My box with accidentals has C, A#/Bb, D#/Eb, and F. Boxes without accidentals on the first button have additional lower notes.

Detailed layouts for different keys and box configurations can be found on *melodeon.net*.

Make sure you know where the air button is on your melodeon. Never push or pull the accordion without having a button down. The air button can be used to quietly open or close the bellows. It can also be used during play to ease quick changes in bellows direction or to get more or less air when need be.

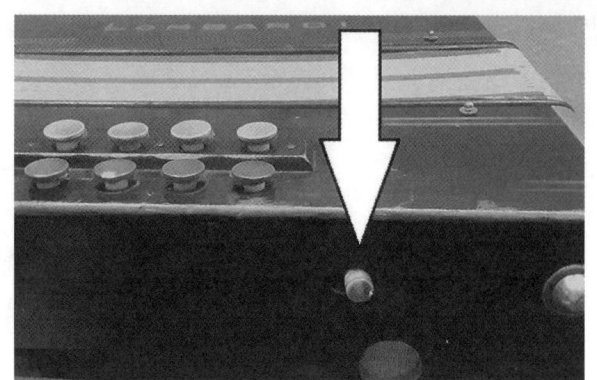

The Bass and Chords

On the left-hand side we have basses and chords. Some two-row boxes will have 12 such buttons, but most have eight. Like the melody buttons, these produce different tones depending on which direction the bellows are moving.

Here is what tones are produced. Remember, this diagram is for an A/D box.

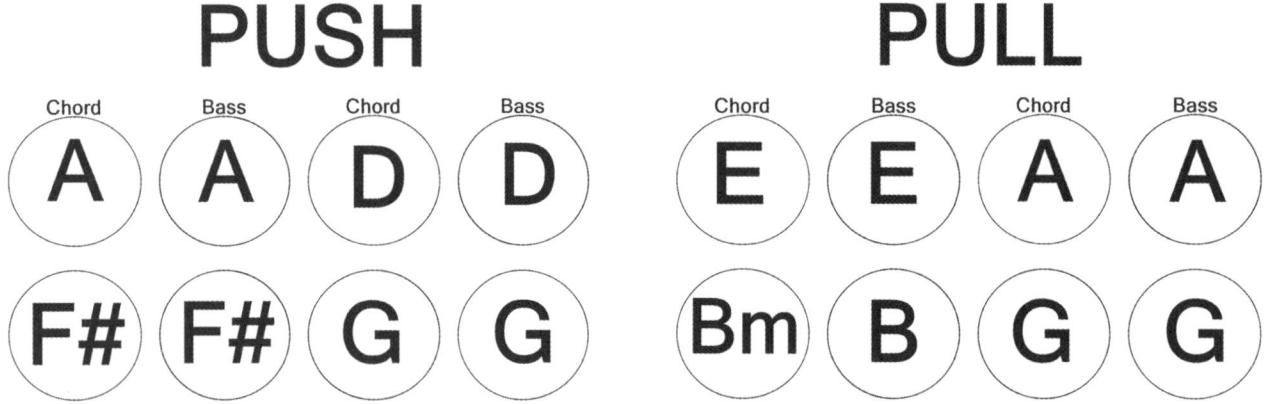

The highlighted buttons below give you a D bass and a D chord when the bellows are pushed. These same buttons give you an A bass and A chord when the bellows are pulled. These are the I and V chords in D. Many one-row boxes, such as those favored in Cajun music, only have these two buttons on the left side.

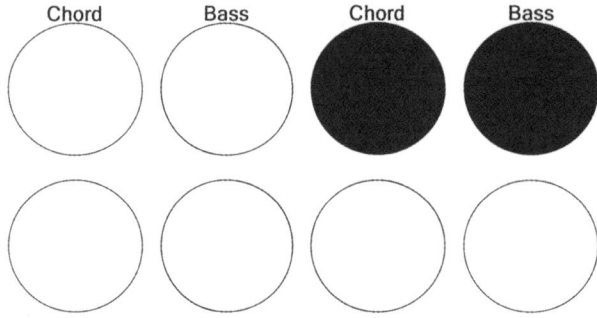

On the other side, we have A and E – the I and V chords for the key of A.

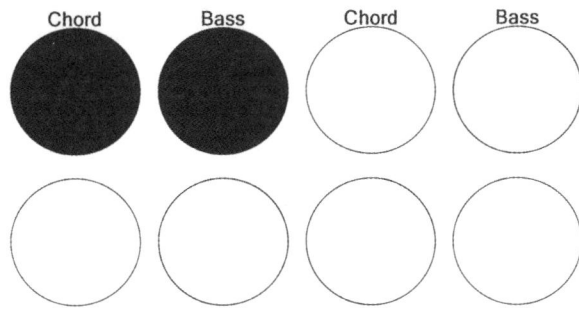

The chords available to you will enable you to accompany songs in the key of D with the I – IV – V – vi chords (D – G – A – Bm). In A, you'll have I – ii – IV – V chords (A – Bm – D – E). There is also the I – V for G (G – D). Many folk songs use just the common I – V and I – IV – V chords.

If you're just starting your accordion journey, I'd encourage you to stick with the two buttons that give you the I – V bass and chords. Utilize them as timekeepers. If you're playing in 4/4 time, play the bass note on beats 1 and 3 and play the chord on beats 2 and 4. Your left hand can become more sophisticated as you become more confident.

On the Tab

The music in this book is written in standard music notation as well as a tablature system. Here is a brief explanation.

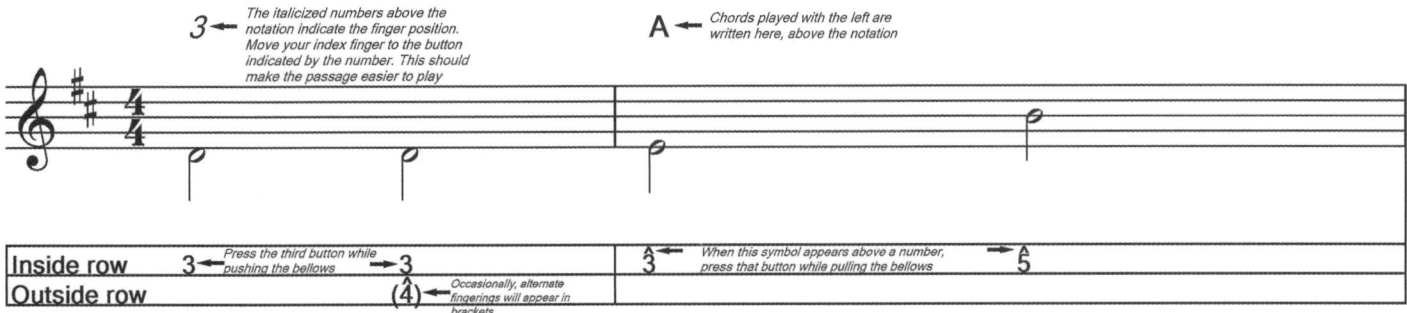

Utilizing this tab, let's play our major scales, first on the outside row (A) and then on the inside row (D). Practicing the scales will help you become familiar with the sounds and movement of the melodeon. Begin with your index finger (finger 1) on the third button. This third button is your home base.

Notice that the 10th button is represented by X. The 11th button, which is on the outside row, will be represented by Y. This is to avoid some confusion. Thankfully, these buttons are seldom used.

A Major Scale

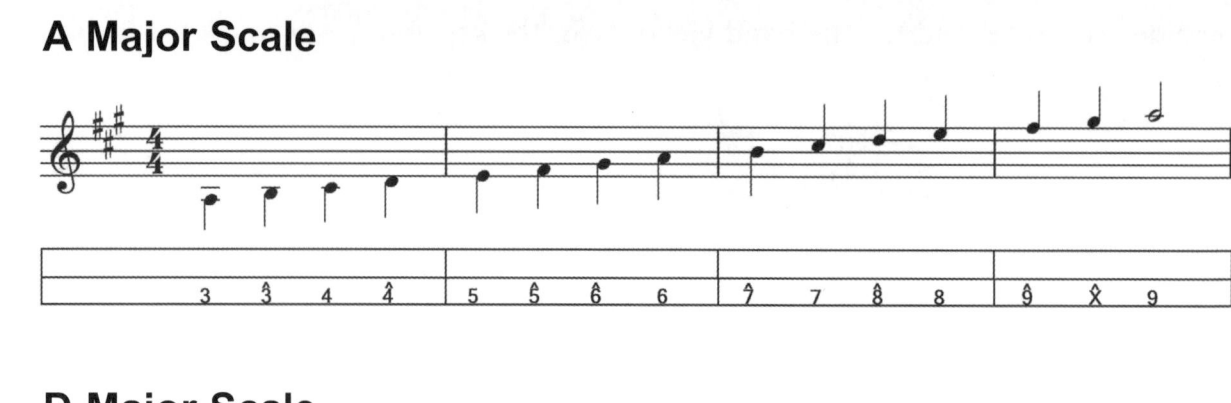

D Major Scale

Be sure to practice these scales both ascending (as is written) and descending (playing it backwards). The more familiar you are with these patterns and sounds, the simpler figuring tunes will become.

Crossing the Rows

Because the two keys are only one note different (the A scale has a G sharp note while the D scale has a G natural) it is possible to use both rows to play melodies. This cross-row technique is common and can make passages easier to play and with less changing in the bellows direction. It may be easier to stick to one row in the beginning, but I encourage you to work on crossing the rows. It pays off quickly.

The diagram below shows the full range of an A/D melodeon with accidentals. Notice where the same notes can be achieved on each row but with a different bellows direction. This knowledge comes in handy!

Remember, the 10th button is represented with an X. The 11th button on the A row is represented by a Y.

The A/D Melodeon's Range

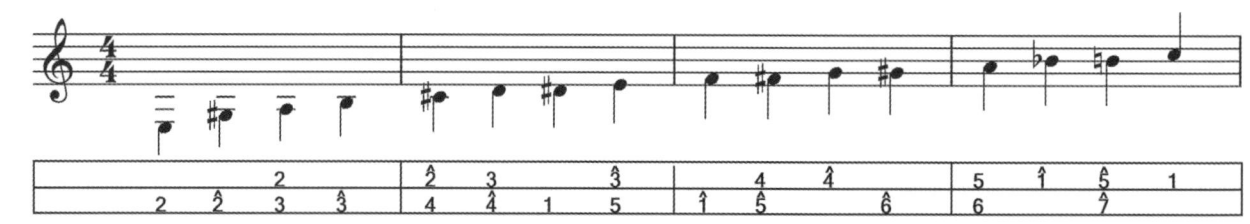

The First Song

Let's get started by taking a simple song. I hope that you are already familiar with the melody *Mary Had a Little Lamb*. First, just play the melody with your right hand.

Mary I

Make sure that you are playing smoothly and steadily. Tap a foot to keep time. Once you can do this, play the same button pattern on the outside row. Doing so will find you playing the *Mary Had a Little Lamb* in the key of A.

Now, let's add bass and chords. Stick with those two buttons that give you the D and A chords. I recommend using your middle finger on the chord button, and your ring finger on the bass button. Before you play the melody along with the bass and chords, try alternating bass – chord – bass – chord while counting steadily to four. Once you can do that, put them together.

Mary II

Once you're comfortable with the coordination between both hands, go on to the third variation of Mary. Here, we add just a little bit of cross-row play, enabling us to hold onto the A chord for beat two in the fourth measure. Also, by using the F# on the outside row, we change the bellows direction and, using our left-hand pointer finger, add the Bm chord.

Mary III

9

Let's explore one final variation. This time, by pressing two buttons, we can add some harmonizing notes. Note that, in the second and fourth measure, you'll have to stretch your pinky finger a little to get that seventh button.

Mary IV

If you can do this, than you're well on your way. Be sure that you continue to experiment.

A Few Notes on Music and Practicing

After many years playing music, I've concluded that there are only four rules that really matter.

1. *If it sounds good to you, it's alright.* Think about it, if you like it, odds are that other people will also like it. Learning theory can help you express what it is you're doing, but sounding good (or finding the bad sound you're looking for) is kinda the point.

2. *Don't work any harder than you have to.* Playing a musical instrument–any musical instrument–is a rare discipline where working harder is to your disadvantage. Small relaxed movements will make for more fluid playing. It may seem counter-intuitive at first, but take my word on this.

3. *If it hurts, you're doing it wrong.* Pain is usually nature's way of telling us to stop. Playing the melodeon can force your fingers to stretch a bit. You may also feel it in your shoulders or arms. If you're hurting, stop and review what you're doing. Fingers hurt from stretching? Maybe look at changing your finger position to better achieve the passage without as much stretching. Shoulders hurt? How are you holding the melodeon?

4. *Once daily practice is a lot better than a lot of practice on one day.* Like everything, the more you do it, the more familiar it becomes. I encourage all students to commit to a 10 minute minimum daily. 10 minutes a day will yield results much quicker than three hours one day a week. If you structure your practice, you'll see even more results. Remember, 10 minutes is the minimum. If you can do more than 10 minutes, do it!

I swear, I'm nearly done. I just want to say a few more things on practicing.

I recommend structuring your time. Remember, 10 minutes minimum. If you're committing to 10 minutes...

- Spend the first two minutes playing exercises
- Spend another three minutes working on a song

- Spend three minutes playing a familiar song
- Always spend time (here, the remaining two minutes) exploring sounds with the instrument. You never know what familiar tune or new invention you'll stumble onto.

Practice should be fun, and when it isn't fun, it should be meditative. Step away if you find yourself frustrated. Maybe it means stepping away from a song you've been working on that just keeps getting the best of you. Maybe it means setting the box down for an hour and going for a walk. Don't add to your frustration by forcing yourself through it. I've never known that to work, personally.

You can play the most complicated piece of music today, provided you play it slowly enough. When practicing, keep good time and keep that good time slow. Playing fast isn't difficult. Speed isn't much more than your comfort and familiarity with what you are doing. I try to remind myself as to how quickly I can tie my shoes. Believe it or not, there was a time when I was learning that it could take me a full five minutes to get those rabbits around the tree.

Remember, actively lis10ing to music is as much practice as anything else. A song comes a lot easier if you can hear it in your head.

The First 10 Songs

I've selected these first 10 songs as they are commonly known among North American Old-Time players. I have ordered them by what I found came easiest to me. That said, each song will provide challenges. It is important to take these slowly. Speed will come. Remember, speed is only your comfort and familiarity with what you are doing. I have added notes to further help. Knowing these 10 songs will give you good starting repertoire.

1. Soldier's Joy

2. Spotted Pony

3. Liberty

4. Angelina Baker

5. Devil's Dream

6. Needle Case

7. Arkansas Traveler

8. Whiskey Before Breakfast

9. Over the Waterfall

10. June Apple

Soldier's Joy

This song is so common that I've found some people will pretend not to know it rather than play it again. That said, it's a fun one on the box and will give you a good opportunity to practice shifting positions. Like many other songs in this book, *Soldier's Joy* is known by other titles including *Love Somebody* and *The King's Head*.

Spotted Pony

I've been told that reversing the A and B sections turns this song into *Snowshoes*. Be sure to take note of when your right hand position changes. There are a number of occasions in this song where the bellows change direction on eighth notes. If I'm playing at a quick tempo, I will have the air button slightly open to make the change easier and not as abrupt sounding.

Liberty

Like *Spotted Pony*, *Liberty* is possible to play on a one-row box. Once you're comfortable with it, try adding some harmonized notes, especially on those quarter notes.

Angelina Baker

Angelina Baker is played entirely out of the fifth position. I have placed asterisks in a couple places in the B section because I will sometimes stay on the bass button, as opposed to going to the chord. If you look at the second measure in the B section, staying on the bass button for the second beat gives you D – A – D – d sequence. If you go to the chord button, you'll have D – a – D – d. Having the A chord on the second beat isn't a big issue, but it can clash if you are playing with someone who is providing accompaniment.

Devil's Dream

Devil's Dream was my goal when I started playing the melodeon. It is challenging and is a real accomplishment once you've got it in your hands. Once you get this version down, see if you can play it an octave higher. My own version has changed through having played it thousands of times. Oftentimes, variations will develop naturally.

Needlecase

I first learned *Needlecase* on the banjo. I often play it alongside *Soldier's Joy*, as the two songs are similar.

Arkansas Traveler

This is the first song in which cross-row playing is necessary. Without it, you cannot get the low B and A notes which are critical to the melody. Thankfully, *Arkansas Traveler* is such a popular tune that there's a good chance you know the melody even if you didn't know its name before.

Whiskey Before Breakfast

More cross-row playing in *Whiskey Before Breakfast*. It is possible to play the E in the first measure by changing bellows direction. Play it both ways and go with what feels and/or sounds best to you.

Over the Waterfall

Over the Waterfall has minimal cross-row fingering. The unique thing about this song is the use of the accidentals, which you can see in the seventh measure of the A section. If your box does not have accidentals, play an E note instead. This, along with the G in the bass, will give you two-thirds of a C major triad.

June Apple

The real challenge with *June Apple* is in keeping the A bass/chord combination. Your left hand will be kept busy with this tune, but this is common with tunes in which utilize the *Mixolydian mode* – where the tonal center is A, but it utilizes the notes associated with the D major scale. Mixolydian encounters are not uncommon in American Old-Time music. It may help you to first become comfortable playing the melody alone before attempting to incorporate the left hand.

Making Arrangements

I wanted to be sure to take some time to write about how to make your own arrangements. These are the steps that I take and I encourage you to try the same. Making your own arrangements will likely become increasingly important to you as you progress as a player. I feel that music is much like writing. Often, it will come naturally and effortlessly flow from you. More often, it is a process and can take a few drafts to get to a place where you are happy.

If you don't already know how to read treble clef, I would encourage you to learn. It will ultimately make things easier and open many musical doors.

If you're looking to make an arrangement, you'll likely refer to a book or a website. There are numerous resources out there. Perhaps you've managed to piece together the notes to a song. Either way, there are considerations specific to the melodeon which ought to inform the decisions we make. Let's look at an excerpt from *Hell Among the Yearlings*.

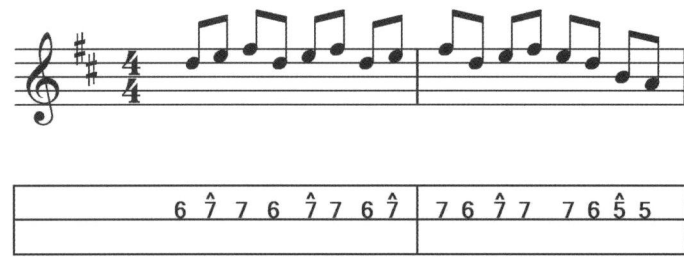

Above, we have the full melody. The melody has been tabbed out for the D row. As you can see, the melody is constant eighth notes and there are some quick bellows movements. You may find it discouraging if you pick up your box and you try to have a go at it as is written. Let's try a few things first.

1. Be sure you know the melody and listen to it a while. Though you can play a song based on the paper itself, it will be much easier if you can hear it in your head.

2. Let's start our draft process by playing only the notes that fall on the beat. This simplifies the arrangement and allows you to get the melody's skeleton in the hands.

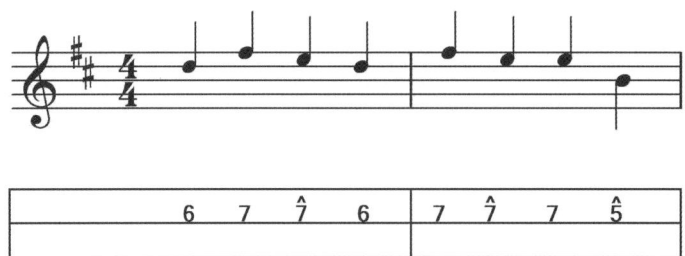

3. While that is certainly simpler, it doesn't really capture the song as we know it. Let's build onto this skeleton by adding the off-beats which do not require a change in bellows direction. Doing so gives us the following draft.

4. The above draft is fuller sounding. You may even be satisfied with it and play this version for years to come. All the same, let us go one step further and utilize the outside row so that we can add off-beat notes which do not require a change in bellows direction.

5. The above arrangement has everything we began with except for the A note which ends the second measure. To get that off-beat note, we would have to change bellows directions quickly. You may choose to do so, or you may choose to leave it as is.

The ideas I've listed can be applied to the arrangements that are in this book. The decisions you make will be influenced by a series of factors, principally the sound and the ease in achieving it. If you are fortunate enough to regularly play music with others, you may choose to stick to a more simplified arrangement, as it works better with the group dynamics. I've been told that the larger the group is, the less any one musician should play, as too much can muddy the waters. I've found this wisdom to be true in most situations. Having written that, I refer back to rule #1: *if it sounds good to you, it's alright!*

You may find that the way you play the tune evolves over time, deviating from something written down. I suggest that this is embraced. The songs in this book have been played by many people over many years and each person plays it slightly differently. For you to have your own take on the song is to put your own link in a long chain that leads all the way back to when it was first played.

Playing in Two Octaves

Many songs stay within an octave, except maybe a few notes. One way we can get more from a song –and add variation –is to work the melody out in both the low and high octaves.

I've selected *Mississippi Sawyer* for this purpose. I've worked out both a low and a high version which play the same notes with the same rhythm – the only musical distinction between the versions is that they are in different octaves.

The lower octave arrangement does not require any right-hand position shifts, but it does require you to utilize the A bass on the push, like we saw in *June Apple*. While both versions have cross-row playing, the high octave version has less. Despite this, I personally find the high octave arrangement to be more challenging for the right hand.

Once you're able to play both versions, experiment with combining them. Maybe you'll start in the low octave, but play the high octave arrangement the second time through the song.

I would encourage you to work out other melodies in both octaves. Doing so not only provides you with more options for variation, but it can help foster a deeper understanding of your instrument.

Mississippi Sawyer (Low Octave)

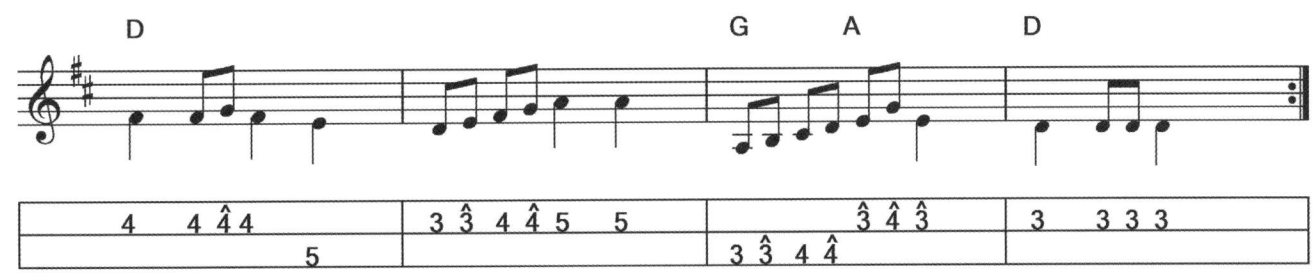

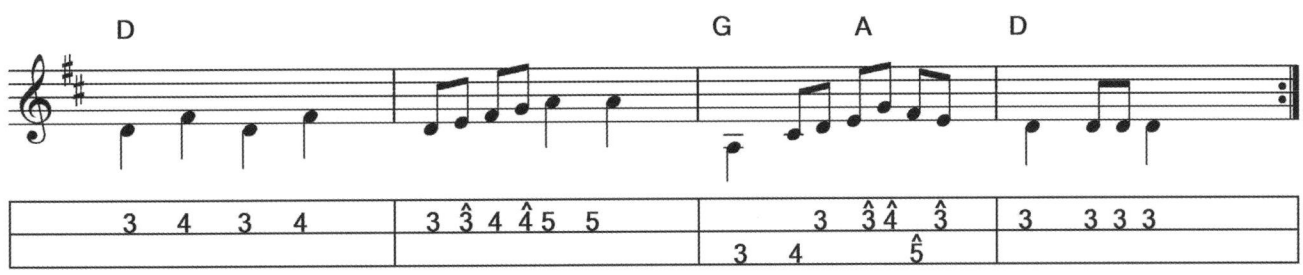

Mississippi Sawyer (High Octave)

Harmonizing Notes

So far, the arrangements have been single note melodies. You may have already experimented with pushing a couple buttons down at a time and found that it worked. When we are playing additional notes alongside the main melody, we are harmonizing that melody. This can be used to add variation to your playing. Some button accordion cultures–such as Slovenian, Austrian, and Cajun–are typically playing two or three notes at once on the melody side.

Let's look at a few examples to better learn what is going on with these harmonized notes. In these examples, the harmonized note will be written smaller, both on the staff and on the tab.

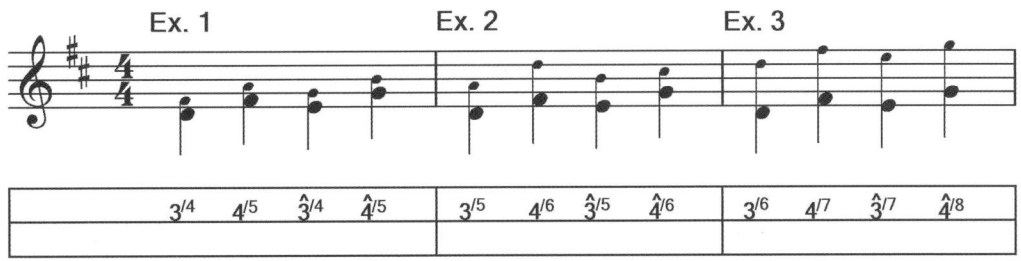

Ex. 1 Here, the harmonized note is one button higher. We are playing in *thirds*. This is because the harmonized note is a third away from the melody note. For example, beat one has us playing a D note. The harmonized note is an F#. Count with your fingers, starting with D (1), then E (2), and landing on F# (3). The distance from one note to another is called an *interval*.

This button relationship remains consistent except for two examples. Try pulling the bellows out with a finger on buttons five and six or nine and 10 on the D row. This will give you a B and C#. This distance, or interval, is a *second*.

Ex. 2 This example has us playing an interval of a *fifth*, with one exception. On beat four, we are playing a G and a C#. The C#, the harmonizing note is a *tritone* and can be called an *augmented fourth* or a *diminished fifth*. Either way, this can be a harmonically challenging sound. If it sounds good to you in a musical context, don't hesitate to use it.

Ex. 3 The final example available to us on a single row is the octave. This is where the same note is played, but one octave higher.

Providing Backup

Many traditional music cultures stick to some common keys. Slovenian style button accordion songs are most often in the keys C, F, and Bb. English Morris players seem to rely on D and G. Southwestern styles tend to favor C, F, and G. The most common keys in American Old-Time are A, D, and G. It goes without saying that there are numerous songs in other keys in the Old-Time tradition, but these tend to be the most common.

I picked up an A/D box due to the how frequently these keys are used in Old-Time. If your box has accidentals, you can have a little more versatility and be able to play some G tunes, but it will be a little more challenging.

If you have a D/G box, another good choice for Old-Time, what I'm saying about the key of G will apply to the key of C.

When playing G tunes alongside a fiddler, I will play some backup ideas with my right hand. I will intersperse these ideas with some melodic runs. Generally, I won't use my left hand, or when I do, it is in a more limited capacity.

Let's start by looking at some chords and *double-stops* (two harmonized notes) which we can use to provide backup on the melodeon.

In the key of G, the diatonic chords (the chords which are made using the notes in a G major scale) include G – Am – Bm – C – D – Em – F#dim. The example below contains three of the more commonly used chords.

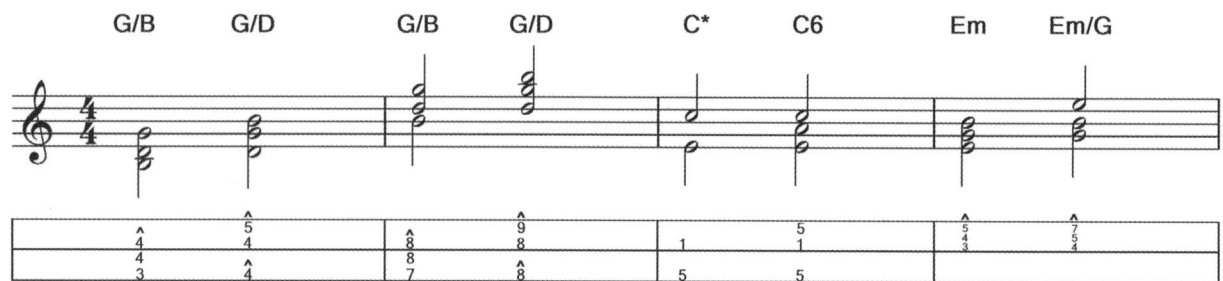

If you are not familiar with some of these names such as G/D, it simply means that you are playing a G chord with a D in the bass. Note the asterisk on the C chord example. This C chord is missing the fifth note (G) and is a double-stop which gives two of the three notes which makes a C major chord.

I did not include the D chord in the above example. Why not? Because pushing any three buttons next to one another on the D row will give you a D major chord, so long as you are pushing the bellows in. The same is true for the A row. If you push the bellows in, while pushing three consecutive buttons, you will get an A major chord.

Common chord progressions include I – V, I – IV – V, and I – vi – IV – V. What does this mean? I've written out a G major scale below.

G	a	b	C	D	e	f#
1	2	3	4	5	6	7

The seven notes above each have a chord associated with them. Again, these are what we refer to as the *diatonic chords*, as they are made using only the notes in this scale. Because the G, C, and D chords are major, I've written them out as uppercase letters. You're likely assuming that the lowercase letters represent minor chords, and you would be correct!

Let's look at those chord progressions though. Progressions are patterns. The first progression I wrote down is the I – V. In other words, take the first chord in G (G major) and the fifth chord (D major). Those are the chords in a I – V progression. Want to play a I – IV – V progression? Just add C, which is the IV chord.

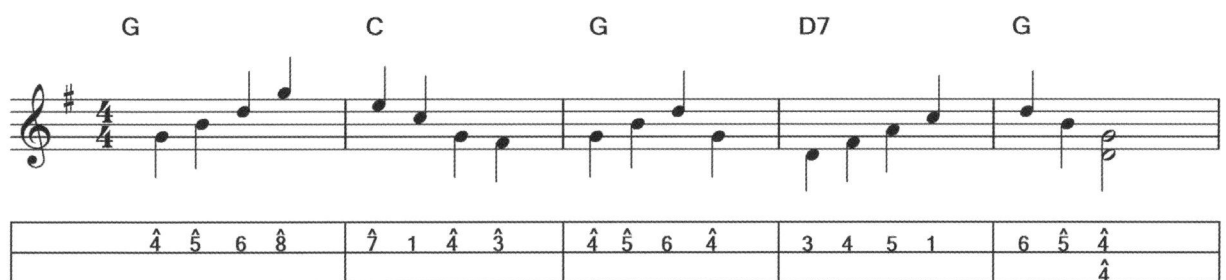

Let's play a I – IV – V chord progression in G. Instead of holding chords down, let's play them as an *arpeggio*. An arpeggio means that we are playing the individual notes as opposed to playing them all at once. Remember, we're not going to play with our left hand. What's more, we don't have a C chord available to us on the A/D box.

Let's wrap this look at chords up by looking at 5ths. These harmonized notes are often known as *Power Chords*. To understand what power chords are, you have to know something about the *major triad* and *minor triad*.

In brief, the recipe to make a major chord is the *major triad*. The major triad is the 1st, 3rd, and 5th note in a scale. If you turn back to the G major scale, these notes will be G(1), B(3), and D(5). The minor triad is almost the same, the only difference being that you flatten the 3rd note. If you replace the B note with a Bb, you'll be playing a G minor chord.

What makes power chords unique and versatile is that they are constructed using only the 1st and 5th notes. Because they lack that 3rd, they are technically neither major nor minor. You can use a power chord in place of a major or a minor chord. Power chords are also known as 5th chords due to their lacking the 3rd.

Next, I've listed all the power chords available on an A/D box. Remember, these can be used as either a major chord or a minor chord.

It is not unusual for some melodeon players tape-down the third note reeds on the left-hand chord buttons. This prevents the third degree from sounding and turns the chords into power chords. This gives a more sparse sound that does give a little more flexibility to the box. This is a personal preference, and you should listen to examples to see what sounds best to you.

Here is an arrangement for *In the Pines*. Here, you will see power chords being used. I have written the accompanying chords above as usual, but try the song without them. Also, try singing the melody and backing yourself up on the accordion using either the left-hand chords, or power chords on the right hand.

In the Pines

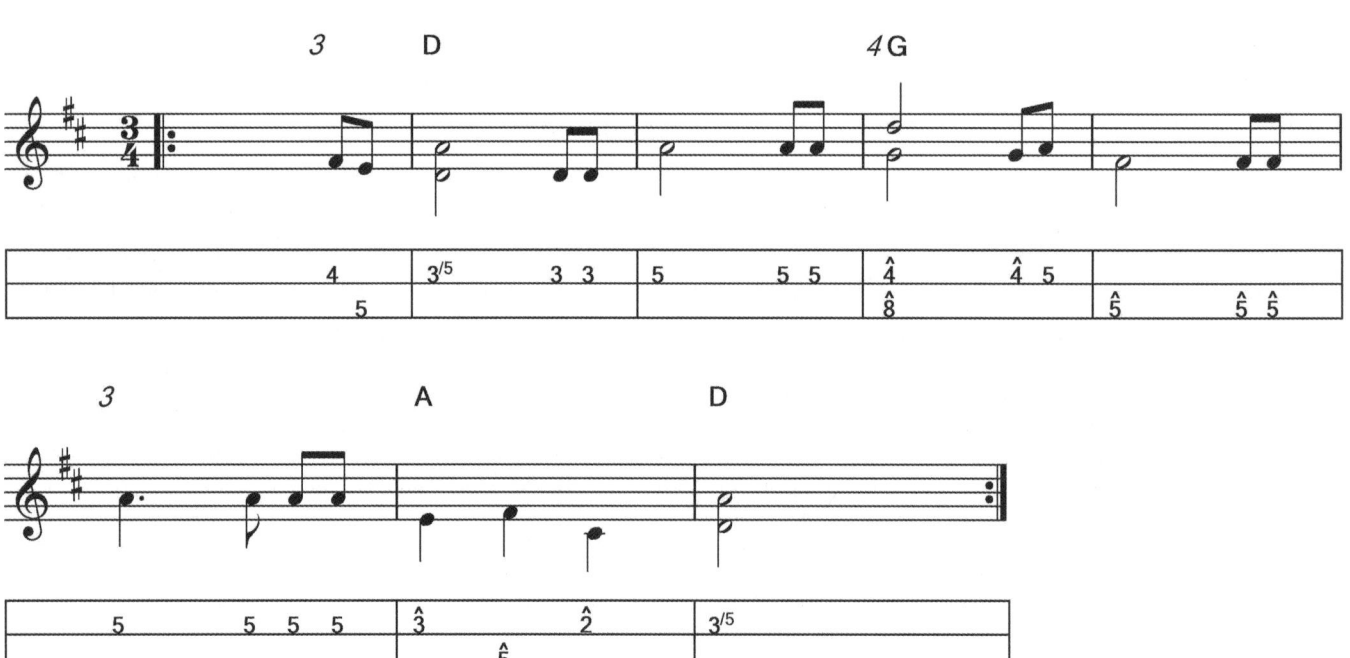

Moving Forward

There are many ways to play the button accordion. What I've presented in this book is only what I've worked out over the years so that I could achieve the songs I wanted to play. I am always learning and enjoying the box. I hope the same for you. I would encourage you to seek out other players and listen to different styles.

The remainder of this book is dedicated to my arrangements of traditional songs played in the United States and Canada. I've added some notes to each song.

I've divided these songs in two categories. The first category is for songs in 4/4. The second category is for 3/4 and 6/8 tunes. 6/8 songs are not common among Old-Time players who focus on the music of Southern Appalachia, but such songs are common enough here in Northern Appalachia and I've included them for the variety, but also because 6/8 songs are common in Celtic music which is a good avenue for further melodeon explorations.

Many of the songs I've selected come from historic Pennsylvanian fiddlers, principally Sarah Armstrong and Irvin Yaugher.

The Blacksmith

This is a Sarah Armstrong tune. Armstrong's influence casts a long shadow over Pennsylvania's fiddle tradition, especially in the western region. The arrangement incorporates some harmonizing notes. In measure seven of the A section, I keep to playing out of the third position, utilizing my fourth finger to stretch to the seventh button.

Buttermilk & Cider

Unlike most of the other songs in this book, *Buttermilk & Cider* does not follow the typical AABB format commonly seen. Rather, this song is played straight through. You'll notice that the second and fourth lines are the same. I would recommend staying in the sixth position through this song and stretch your fourth finger to get the notes in on the tenth button.

Dubuque

It is my understanding that this tune comes from the Midwest. I was first introduced to it at a jam in Western Pennsylvania. I've come to be most familiar with Bob Walter's 1955 recording where he is accompanied by a pianist. Playing this song on the melodeon is not too hard, there is minimal cross-row play. The challenge is being able to play it quickly and cleanly. That said, this melody sounds good at any speed.

Forked Deer

Forked Deer is a song that goes way back. I believe it was first recorded in 1929 by Charlie Bowman who recorded it for Columbia with the title *Forky Deer*. Bowman's version was more involved than the two sections I have transcribed above. It is common to hear a third section and I would recommend you to take your hand at transcribing a third section.

Hang On

Hang On is another Pennsylvanian tune and comes to us from Irvin Yaugher. Yaugher spent years as a miner, gunsmith, and fiddler. This compact song is not too challenging, except for the triplets which start each section. To help achieve these, I leave my air valve slightly open. You can also drop the middle note in the triplet pattern and play the two notes as a pair of eighth notes instead.

A quick note on the chords: in the final measure of both the A and B sections, you will be pulling the bellows out on beat one, which will find you playing the A bass on your left hand. Not to worry! The A note is part of a D major chord and having an A in the bass will not sound jarring.

Lamplighter's Hornpipe

Lamplighter's Hornpipe has been my favorite to play for some time. Traditionally, a hornpipe is played with a syncopated long-short rhythm. Many American players straighten it out so that it sounds like a reel. Getting the syncopation can be tricky, especially when you're developing coordination with your right and left hands.

League & Slasher Reel

I forget where I first encountered this song, but I believe it was in a collection of fiddle tunes. My arrangement has dropped some of the off-beats so that it flows a bit better. I selected to include this song as, like *June Apple*, it is in A Mixolydian. The Mixolydian mode can be thought of in several ways, but I tend to think of it as playing a scale starting and ending on the fifth note in that scale. For example, a D scale is played D-E-F#-G-A-B-C#. Here, A is the fifth note in the scale. An A Mixolydian scale is therefore played A-B-C#-D-E-F#-G, which is essentially a normal A Major Scale, but with the seventh note (G#) lowered.

Little Hornpipe

From Sarah Armstrong, this song incorporates some cross-row playing in order to limit rapid bellows changes. Also, note that you will have to move your left hand a bit in order to get you A bass on the push.

Sweet Ellen

This is another Irvin Yaugher song. In Samuel Bayard's *Hill Country Tunes*, it is noted that the song's origins are likely Irish.

Lady on the Railroad

A while back, my friend Holly sent some older music books my way. This song came from *The Universal Favorite Contra Dance Album*, published in 1901. This album was compiled for orchestra and many well-known songs such as *Devil's Dream, Lamplighter's Hornpipe*, and *Paddy on the Turnpike* can be found inside its yellowed pages. I'd assumed that this song was just a version of *Jenny on the Railroad*, but that does not sound to be the case to me.

There are opportunities for cross-row playing the B section which could help reduce frequent changes in the bellow's directions. I left those out as I find it simpler to stick on the one row for the B section.

Breaking Up Christmas

Breaking Up Christmas is said to come to us from "Old Man" Pet McKinney, a Civil War Veteran who would influence fiddlers in the area of Round Peak. These players, including Tommy Jarrell, would go on to become seminal figures in Appalachian music.

Snowflake Hornpipe

A friend sent me their transcription of this tune, and I've adapted it here for the button accordion. As I recall, they picked it up from some sessions in Texas.

Snouts & Ears of America

Snouts & Ears of America comes from Pennsylvania fiddler Sarah Armstrong. Though this is based on her playing, I've been told that this song originates in Scotland.

Young America Hornpipe

This hornpipe takes us all the way up the fingerboard, playing out of the seventh position. For me, it took a while to become comfortable playing in the higher octave. Be sure to take this one slowly.

Whiskey

Another Irvin Younger tune, this is a case where we can play a G tune without much difficulty on an A/D box. How is this? Because the tune does not use a C natural note. Both our A and D scales have a C# in them. Although an A/D box with accidentals has a C natural, it isn't always easy to get as it can demand a quick position change with your right hand.

Songs in G which use the *major pentatonic scale* (G – a – b – D – e) are good candidates for G tunes on the A/D. Whiskey uses an occasional f#, and so the melody could be said to utilize a *hexatonic scale*. The pentatonic scale has five tones, and the hexatonic has six.

You'll note that I rotate between the third and fourth position. I stretch my fourth finger out in order to get the 8th button for that high G note.

Bunch of Keys

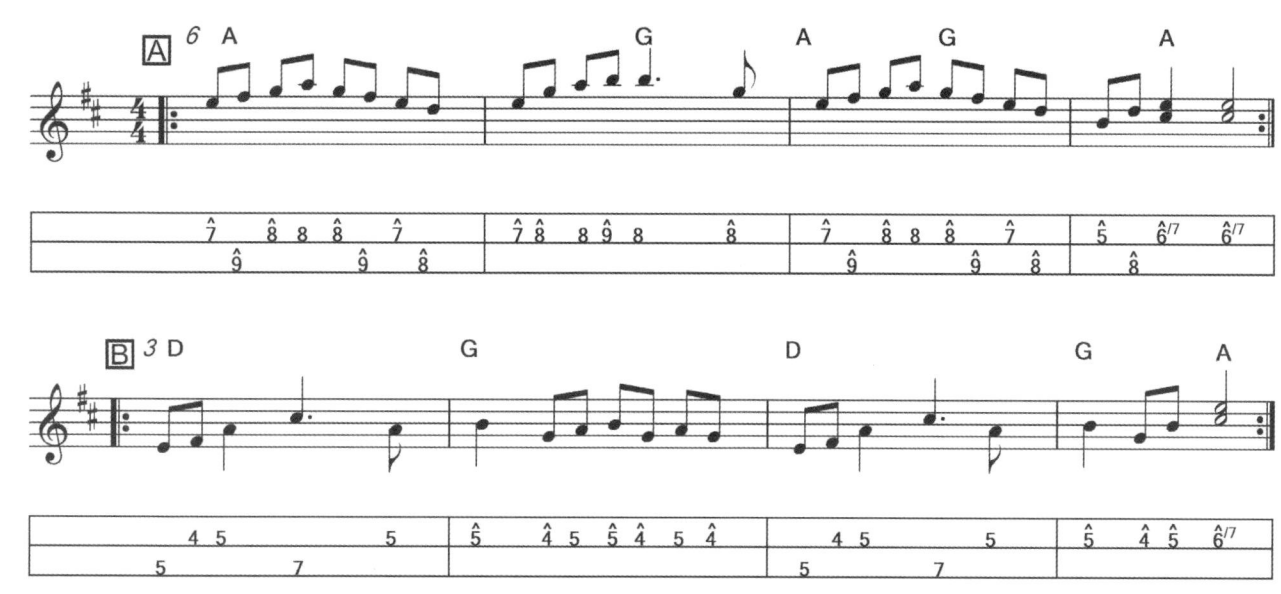

Another Mixolydian tune, I'm most familiar with a recording Tommy Jarrell made with Paul Brown on banjo. This recording is available from *The Field Recorders' Collective*.

Jigs and Waltzes

These final few songs are jigs (most often 6/8 time) and even a waltz (3/4 time). Jigs are not terribly common to the player most familiar with the Southern Appalachian fiddling culture, but jigs and waltz can be found in the northern regions.

I wanted to give a few tips on the left hand for the next few numbers.

With the waltz, my approach has been simple and straightforward:

Count: 1-Bass   2-Chord   3-Chord

Jigs once presented me with a dilemma that took me a while to sort out. There are a few ways you can count a jig's six beats

The second example works best for me when playing a string instrument. That said, it didn't help me when I was working on the bass hand on a jig.

I've taken to counting like the third example above. You can think of it as playing triplets in 2/4 time. Counting a jig like this, at least on the melodeon, helped me get the left hand engaged.

Count: 1-Bass - pa - let   2-Chord - pa - let

Sometimes, I'll hold the chord button down a little longer than the beat. As always, this is just what worked for me and other people play it differently. See what works for you.

Some people encouraged me to learn the melody solid before adding the left hand. Others told me that I should work on both hands at once so that I more quickly internalize the motion and rhythm. Both suggestions have their points, but the latter worked for me. Clearly, people learn differently. If you're trying to work both hands out but struggling to make headway, maybe getting comfortable with the melody first will work better for you.

The Kesh Jig

A popular jig at Celtic sessions, there are many ways to approach the A section, but I choose this way so that I do not run the risk of running out of room with the bellows. Notice that this is another tune we can play in G, as there are no C notes in the song.

John Newgrant Came Home with a Pain in His Head

Yet another tune from Sarah Armstrong. As I've written before, it seems that jigs become more common the further north one travels. Pennsylvania seems to have maintained more 6/8 tunes than other Appalachian states. I do not have a hypothesis as to why, but I have wondered if fife and drum bands which were recently more common in the area helped to reinforce and maintain the jig.

St. Lawrence Jig

I forget where I first encountered this song, but I've always had a place in my heart for the St. Lawrence River, despite a large fish nearly tipping my canoe over while I fished on its waters as a child. Regardless, I associate this with summer in Quebec.

The Merry Widow

I do not know much about this tune. I found a handwritten transcription amid a friend's notes. They said it is related to an operetta of the same name, and though I know the operetta exists, I have not been able to confirm if this melody has anything to do with the 1905 operetta or its 1918 celluloid counterpart.

Amazing Grace

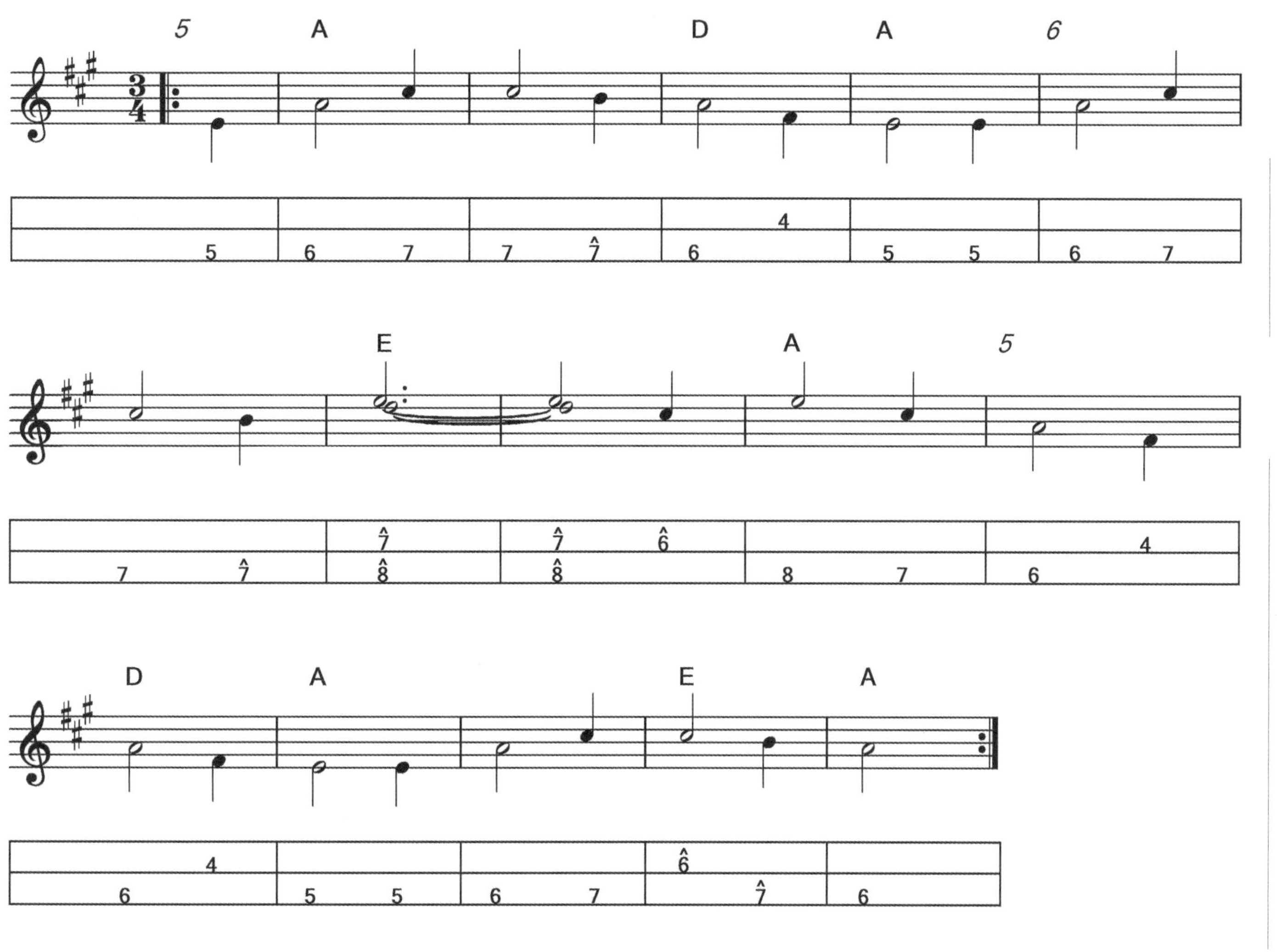

Amazing Grace is as good as any song I can think to end with. Be sure to start with a good bit of air and play it with feeling. I often play it without the left hand for a sparser sound.

Conclusion

I hope that this book has helped you in your musical journey. I wish for you continued growth and enjoyment with the melodeon, and I hope that you feel capable and encouraged to make your own arrangements of the songs that you enjoy listening to. As you play, lean into the things that give you your own style.

There is always more to discover, and I know that my own learning will continue. I look forward to this, despite realizing that it means there will be things I regret not writing down in this book. But that's the way it is, and maybe I'll put fingers to the keyboard once more in the future.

Musically yours,

Nic "Pennsylvania" Landon

NEW FROM Centerstream

You'll Like What You Hear

THE IRISH TENOR BANJO
by Dick Sheridan
00370212............................ $19.99

EASY CHORDS SOLOS FOR GUITAR
by Dick Sheridan
00364942............................ $19.99

GOLDTOP BELIEVERS
by Vic Da Pra & David Plues
00368381............................ $85.00

PARLOR, PORCHES & ISLANDS
by Doc Rossi
00363751............................ $19.99

UKULELE SONGS AROUND THE WORLD
by Dick Sheridan
00360589............................ $15.99

BURST BELIEVERS V
by Vic Da Pra & David Plues
00350746............................ $85.00

LOW G TUNING FOR THE UKULELE
by Dick Sheridan
00362325............................ $19.99

HOT SPICY TRUMPET SOLOS
by Gerald F. Knipfel
00329680............................ $19.99

EARLY PETE SEEGER BANJO TECHNIQUES
by Joseph Weildlich
00381542............................ $19.99

DECONSTRUCTING PRODUCTION MUSIC FOR TV
by Steve Barden
00367071............................ $24.99

MASTERING STAFFPAD
by Steve Barden
00354792............................ $29.99

OLD-TIME RADIO MUSIC THEMES FOR UKULELE
by Dick Sheridan
00398136............................ $19.99

ORDER TODAY! Call **1-714-779-9390** • orders@centerstream-usa.com • Distributed by Hal Leonard